Mimi's Garden

Written & Illustrated
by
Martha M. Cooper

Copyright © 2009 by Martha M. Cooper
Revised 2012
All rights reserved.
No part of this book may be reproduced without
written permission.

ISBN-13: 978-1442124622
ISBN-10: 1442124628

Photographs and illustrations by
Martha M. Cooper

Raccoon photo used with permission of
Patricia M. Bips

For

Hazel, Anna, Bailey, Ben & Matt

Come see the creatures in Mimi's Garden

Look!
A spider is on the
Yellow flower!

This lizard is a
Green Anole

He can change color
from green ...

...to brown

To hide he changed his color to green ...

Can you find him?

The Gray Rat Snake is another reptile that can hide.

He is the same color as the tree branch.

Here is a butterfly on a purple flower.

We can see the life cycle
of a butterfly in Mimi's Garden.

The butterfly lays her
eggs on a leaf.

A caterpillar hatches
from an egg and starts
to eat the leaf.

She eats and eats and...

...eats!

And gets bigger
and bigger.
Then she spins into a chrysalis.

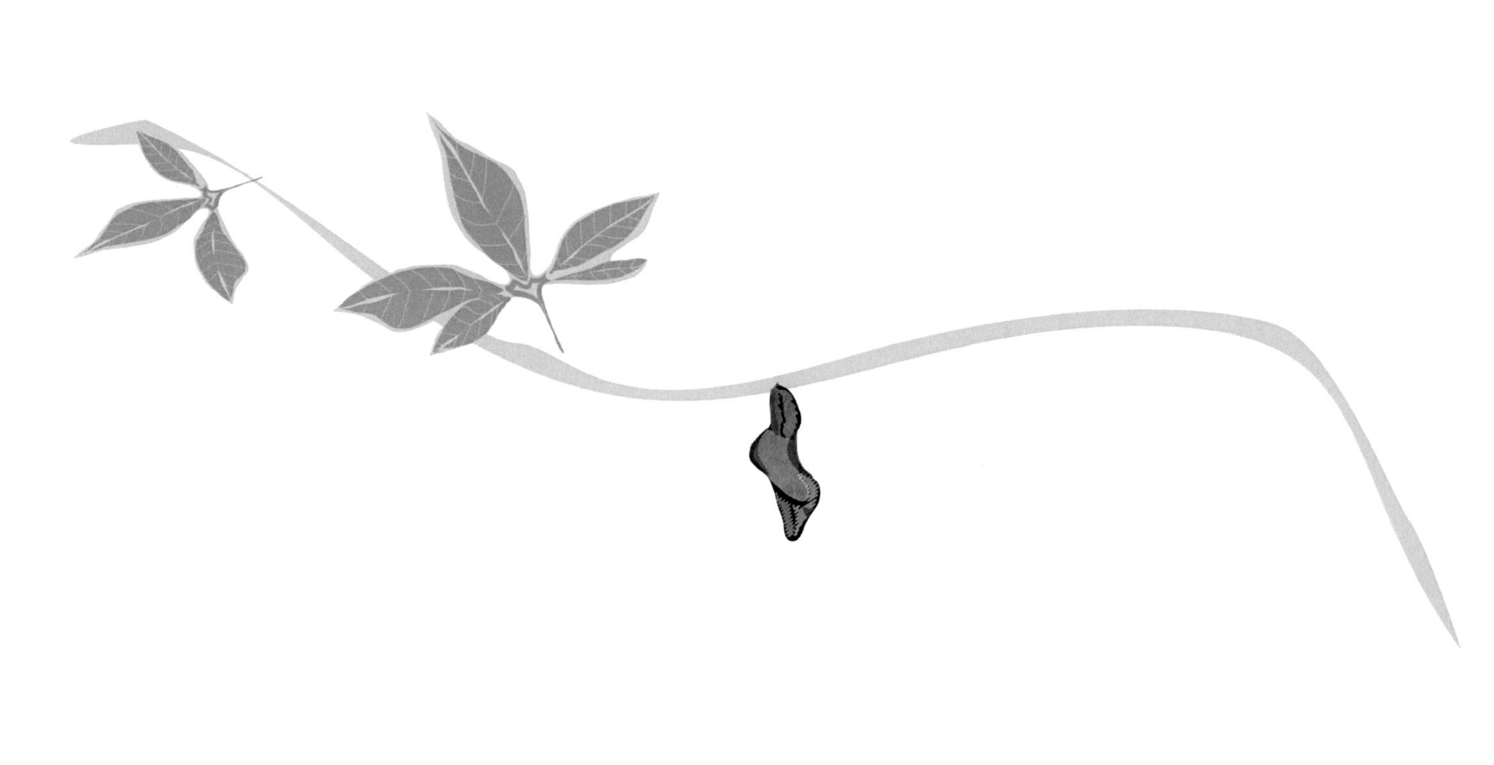

In a few days she will come out as a beautiful butterfly.

The red ladybug
eats bugs in
Mimi's Garden.

The little green tree frog
waits to catch
bugs too.

Here is the tree frog
on the window.

This dragonfly is
looking for mosquitos
to eat.

What is the kitty looking for in the garden?

The bee has found some
pollen on the
red Hibiscus flower.

Mimi feeds the birds
in the garden.

The Blue Jay is looking for
some seeds to eat.....

and the Cardinal
is taking a
bird bath.

At night this
raccoon eats the food
Mimi put in the garden
for the birds.

She is not very nice.

This is a gopher tortoise,
a land turtle that
lives in a burrow.

There are even more
bugs in the garden!

This Praying Mantis is looking
for other bugs to eat.

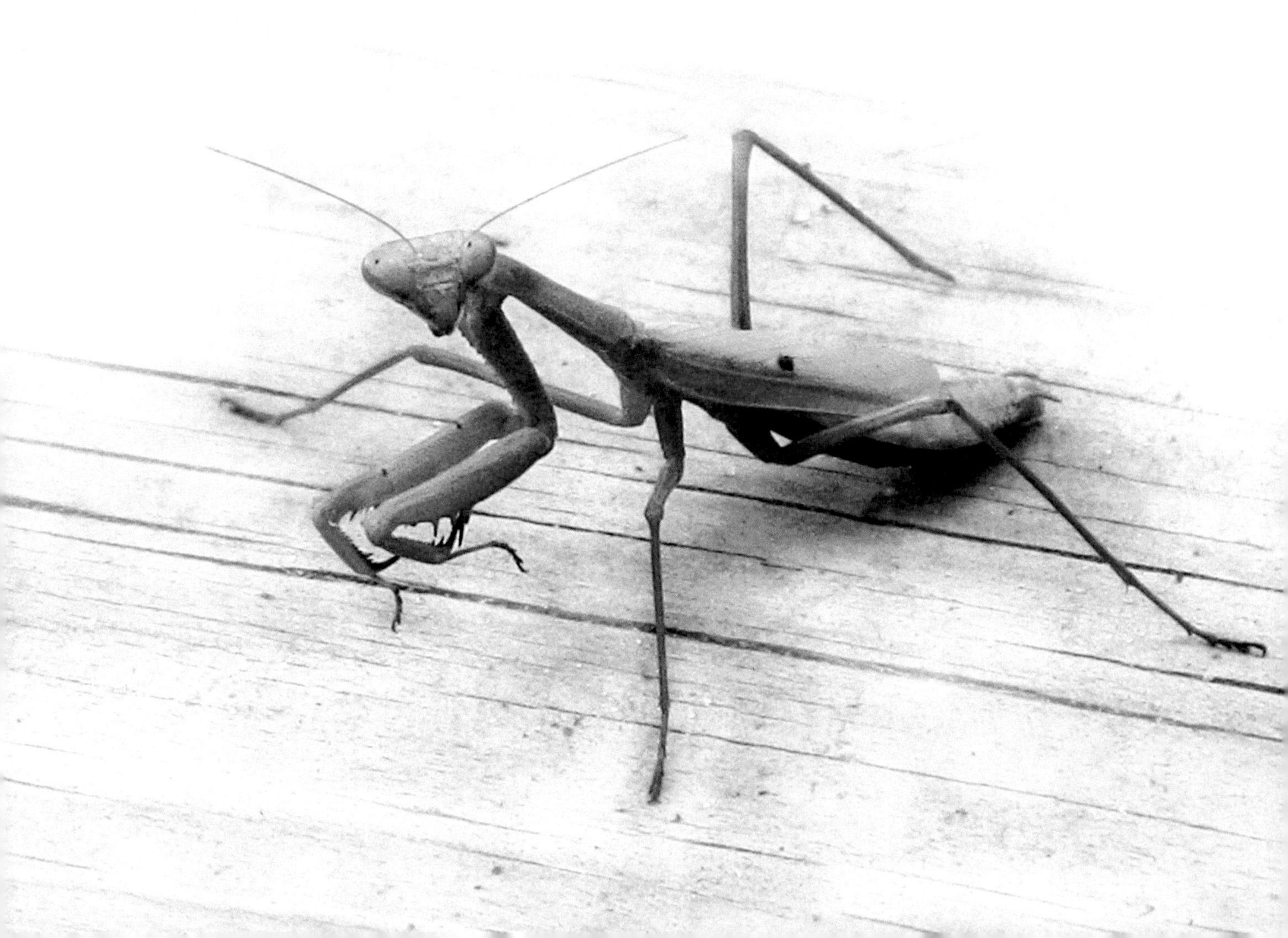

And this one is called
a Walking Stick.

Don't touch her or she
might spray a stinky
smell on you.

Look at the pretty colors
on this lizard.

He is a Blue Skink.

You never know what you
will see in Mimi's Garden.

Sometimes you
may even see a glimpse
of the quick Gray Fox.

There are all kinds of wild and crawly things to see in Mimi's Garden.

Made in the USA
San Bernardino, CA
18 December 2016